PETS' GUIDES

Ruff's Guide to

Caring
for Your
Dog

Anita Ganeri

Raintree

KT-428-243

04219829

Raintree is an imprint of Capstone Global Library Limited, a company incorporated in England and Wales having its registered office at 7 Pilgrim Street, London, EC4V 6LB– Registered company number: 6695582

To contact Raintree:
Phone: 0845 6044371
Fax: + 44 (0) 1865 312263
Email: myorders@raintreepublishers.co.uk
Outside the UK please telephone +44 1865 312262

Text © Capstone Global Library Limited 2013
First published in hardback in 2013
First published in paperback in 2014
The moral rights of the proprietor have been asserted.

All rights reserved. No part of this publication may be reproduced in any form or by any means (including photocopying or storing it in any medium by electronic means and whether or not transiently or incidentally to some other use of this publication) without the written permission of the copyright owner, except in accordance with the provisions of the Copyright, Designs and Patents Act 1988 or under the terms of a licence issued by the Copyright Licensing Agency, Saffron House, 6–10 Kirby Street, London EC1N 8TS (www.cla.co.uk). Applications for the copyright owner's written permission should be addressed to the publisher.

Edited by Daniel Nunn, Rebecca Rissman, and Sian Smith
Designed by Cynthia Della-Rovere
Picture research by Tracy Cummins
Original illustrations © Capstone Global Library Ltd 2013
Illustrated by Rick Peterson
Production by Victoria Fitzgerald
Originated by Capstone Global Library Ltd
Printed and bound in China by South China Printing Company Ltd

ISBN 978 1 4062 5058 9 (hardback)
16 15 14 13 12
10 9 8 7 6 5 4 3 2 1

ISBN 978 1 4062 5065 7 (paperback)
17 16 15 14 13
10 9 8 7 6 5 4 3 2 1

British Library Cataloguing in Publication Data
Ganeri, Anita, 1961-
Ruff's guide to caring for your dog. – (Pets' guides)
   1. Dogs–Juvenile literature.
   I. Title II. Series
   636.7-dc23

Acknowledgements
The author and publisher are grateful to the following for permission to reproduce copyright material: Alamy p. 27 (© blickwinkel); Capstone Library p. 7 (Karon Dubke); Corbis p. 25 (© Larry Williams Associates); Getty Images pp. 9 (Thinkstock Images), 13 (Meg Takamura), 17 left (Steve Lyne), 21 (John Howard); iStockphoto p. 5 (© kristian sekulic); Photoshot p. 23 (© BSIP); Shutterstock pp. 11 (© Cheryl E. Davis), 15 (© Will Hughes), 17 right (© Alis Photo), 19 (© lifeandlove).

Cover photograph of a Jack Russell terrier reproduced with permission of Corbis (© Mike Watson/moodboard). Design elements reproduced with permission of Shutterstock (© Picsfive) and Shutterstock (© R-studio).

We would like to thank Caroline Kisko, Communications Director at the Kennel Club, for her assistance in the preparation of this book.

Every effort has been made to contact copyright holders of material reproduced in this book. Any omissions will be rectified in subsequent printings if notice is given to the publisher.

Disclaimer
All the Internet addresses (URLs) given in this book were valid at the time of going to press. However, due to the dynamic nature of the Internet, some addresses may have changed, or sites may have changed or ceased to exist since publication. While the author and Publishers regret any inconvenience this may cause readers, no responsibility for any such changes can be accepted by either the author or the Publishers.

Contents

Some words are shown in bold, **like this**. You can find out what they mean by looking in the glossary.

Do you want a pet dog?

Hi! I'm Ruff the dog, and this book is all about dogs like me. Did you know that dogs make brilliant pets? We're fun to take for walks and we're great company. In return, you need to look after us properly for the whole of our lives.

Being a good dog owner means making sure that I'm always cared for. I need a safe place to live, food, water, and plenty of exercise. Then I'll quickly become your best friend.

Choosing your dog

We dogs come in many different sizes, colours, and **breeds**. The best places to get your new pet are from an animal shelter or a good **dog breeder**. When buying a puppy, it is a good idea to watch it with its mother and see how it behaves.

Do you want a dog or a puppy? Puppies are lots of fun but you have to train them and spend lots of time with them. It isn't fair to get a puppy otherwise. You might want to pick an older dog like me instead.

A healthy dog

Make sure that the dog you choose is lively and healthy, like me. Look at my shiny coat and clear, bright eyes. My nose is cold and wet. That's another sign that I am healthy.

Some dogs are very playful. Other dogs are quiet and gentle. Think about your family when you choose a dog. A shy dog might not like living in a noisy, busy house.

Getting ready

Before you bring me home, get a few things ready. You need dog food, bowls for my food and water, a brush, some toys, and a collar and **tag**. The tag should have your family's name and address on it in case I get lost, or ask your vet about fitting a **microchip**.

I also need a cosy bed to sleep in with a blanket or soft padding. Plastic, chew-proof beds are best, especially for puppies. Put my bed somewhere warm and quiet where I won't be disturbed if I need a rest.

Welcome home

My new home will feel strange at first but I'll quickly settle in. When I arrive, show me where my bed is and leave me for a while to get used to it. Keep me in one room to begin with, so that I don't get scared. Then let me explore more of the house.

I should get on fine with other pets, once I get to know them. Many dogs live happily with other dogs and cats. Introduce me to them gently and don't leave us alone together at first. After a while, we should become friends.

Feeding time

Woof! Woof! It's dinner time and I'm hungry. I need food and water every day to keep me fit and healthy. You can feed me on dry or wet dog food. Dry food is better for my teeth. You can buy this from the pet shop or supermarket.

Ruff's top meal-time tips

 Adult dogs like me need two meals a day. Puppies need three to four smaller meals.

 Some human foods, such as chocolate, raisins, and onions, are poisonous to dogs.

 Make sure that I always have clean, fresh water to drink.

 Don't feed me too many treats. They can make me overweight and unhealthy.

 Sometimes give me a chewy bone to help clean my teeth.

Exercise

Dogs like me are energetic animals and like lots of exercise. I need to go for a walk or run twice a day. Otherwise, I'll get bored and unfit. Puppies can't go for walks until they have had their first **vaccinations** to stop them catching diseases.

Be careful not to touch dog's mess with your hands, and always wash your hands after picking it up.

Keep me on my lead until it is safe to let me off. Make sure that you clear up any dog mess if I go to the toilet. Use a bag to pick up the mess and put it in the bin.

Training

Like all dogs, I need to be trained. You can train me at home or take me to a training class. Teach me to come when you call my name and to sit when you tell me to. Never shout at or hit your dog. It will make it nervous and scared.

Puppies need to be **toilet trained**. They have to learn to go to the toilet outside. Put your puppy outside every hour and every time it wakes up or after a meal. It will soon learn that going outside means going to the toilet.

Play time

I love to play! My favourite game is fetching a ball. You can buy dog toys from a pet shop, but make sure that they are not too small. I especially like toys that I can chew. If I crouch down low on my front legs, it means that I'm ready to play.

I also like being stroked and patted, especially around my ears and on my chest. If I'm happy, I'll wag my tail. But if I growl or grumble, I want to be left alone. Never pester me while I'm having my dinner or having a nap in my bed.

Coat care

Keep my coat in top condition by **grooming** me every day. This keeps my coat clean and shiny and gets rid of any old hairs. You can buy special grooming brushes from a pet shop. If I have long hair, you might need to get it **clipped**.

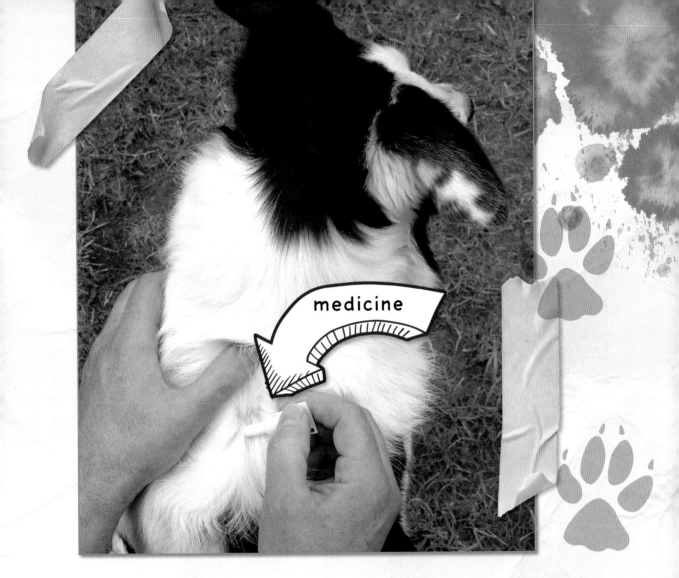

medicine

You need to check my coat regularly in case I have **fleas**. Look for dark specks on my skin. Then treat me with medicine from the vet. You also need to give me medicine to help get rid of **worms**.

Visit to the vet

As soon as I come to live with you, take me to the vet for a check-up. Then, take me once a year for **vaccinations** to keep me healthy. Please also take me to the vet if I go off my food or don't seem well.

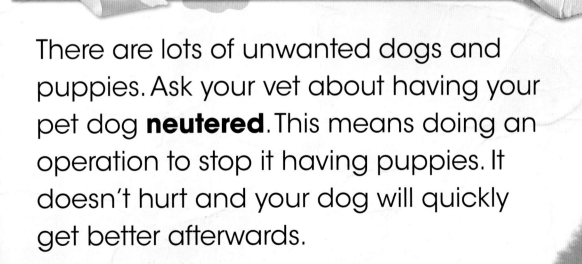

There are lots of unwanted dogs and puppies. Ask your vet about having your pet dog **neutered**. This means doing an operation to stop it having puppies. It doesn't hurt and your dog will quickly get better afterwards.

Happy holidays

If you go on holiday, you might be able to take me with you. Don't forget to pack my bed, bowls, lead, and toys. If you are driving a long way in the car, keep stopping to let me have a drink and go to the toilet.

If you can't take me with you, please don't just leave me at home alone. Ask a friend or neighbour to stay with me or take me to their home. Otherwise, you could put me in a **boarding kennel**. It is like a hotel for dogs.

Dog facts

 Pet dogs are all related to wolves. Wolves were probably first kept as pets about 15,000 years ago.

 There are more than 400 **breeds** of pet dog, from tiny Chihuahuas to enormous St Bernards.

 Dogs have an amazing sense of smell. They can smell about a million times better than humans.

Dogs can be trained to help people who are blind or deaf. Rescue dogs help to find people after disasters, such as earthquakes.

Helpful tips

 If you have more than one dog, make sure that each has its own bed, toys, and food and water bowls to stop them fighting.

 Your dog must always have a safe, quiet place where it can hide away if it feels scared.

 Don't leave a dog on its own for too long. Dogs like company and they can get bored and lonely.

Don't leave a dog in a car on a warm day, even with a window open. It can quickly get too hot and may die.

Glossary

boarding kennel a place where you can leave your dog when you go on holiday

breeds different types of dogs or other animals

clipped when a dog's coat is cut so that it is short and tidy

dog breeder a person who has puppies or dogs looking for new homes

fleas tiny insects that can live on a dog

grooming brushing or cleaning your dog's coat

microchip a tiny chip that is put under a dog's skin. It has a special number that can be read by a scanner if the dog gets lost.

neutered when a dog has an operation so that it cannot have puppies

tag a metal circle that fixes to a dog's collar

toilet trained when a dog is taught to go to the toilet outside

vaccinations medicines given through a needle by a vet to stop dogs catching diseases

worms worms that grow inside your dog and can make it ill

Find out more

Books to read

Dog (Collins Family Pet Guide), David Sands
  (Collins, 2011)

Dogs (Pets Plus), Sally Morgan (Franklin Watts, 2011)

Websites

www.dogstrust.org.uk
The Dogs Trust in the UK is a charity that looks after stray and abandoned dogs and helps to find homes for them.

www.rspca.org.uk/home
Find out about how to care for your pet on the RSPCA's website.

www.thekennelclub.org.uk
On this website, you can read about every different breed of dog.

Index